Graceful Reflection

The Book of I Am

James Editor Brinson

Copyright @ 2019 by Sirius Gold Media, LLC

All rights reserved, including the right to reproduce this book or portions thereof in any form whatsoever without written permission except in the case of reprints in the context of reviews.

Sirius Gold Media, LLC
www.siriusgoldmedia.com

www.jameseditor.com

ISBN: 978-1-7344331-0-4 (eBook)
ISBN: 978-1-7344331-1-1 (print)

Library of Congress Control Number: 2020930039

Photographs and Design by James Editor Brinson

For information about special discounts for bulk purchases, please email Publisher Sirius Gold Media at info@siriusgoldmedia.com.

Gratitude for

Spirit,

Ancestors,

Mother, Father,

Sister, Brother,

Niece,

Aunts, Uncles,

Cousins,

Goddaughters,

Friends,

Intimate Partners,

Sri Amma Bhagavan,

Atma Nambi

&

Circle of Sacred Nature

Contents

Introduction	1
Tips	3
Reflection through Self	5
Reflection through Love	45
Reflection through God	77

Introduction

I was born and raised in New Orleans, but the city and area never felt like home. After a continual series of disappointments, I was determined to travel the world to find where I belong. In my young adult life, I moved back and forth, switching jobs, meeting new people, encountering different paths and partnerships. Finally in 2011, during a short visit, a gut intuition told me to be open to staying in New Orleans. I decided to listen to the intuitive message, and at the pivotal age of thirty, I moved back to New Orleans with no game plan and open to the Universal Calling.

After a year in the city, I desperately needed a new way of life. I found a local meditation group, which was another turning point in my Journey. Two aspects of the group resonated deeply; a belief that the Outer World is a reflection of the Inner World, and to simply be with my emotions. In hindsight, I realized I had been running away from memories, connections, emotions, and myself. The third appealing aspect was the act of Inviting in Grace; to simply Be with myself as I am and invite in grace.

This book is a result of sitting with the Self and inviting in Grace. This is a collection of reflections, tears, laughter, clarity, and epiphanies, combined with photographs acquired during my travels of a region I once was desperate to leave. By listening to intuition, my life has shifted.

The intention within this book is the sharing
of Divine Purpose.

Graceful Reflection

James Editor Brinson

Tips

Ways to utilize the book.

1. Read traditionally from beginning to end.
2. Read by selecting a page at random.
3. Select a message a day to reflect on.
4. Read with a journal and write about any feelings or thoughts that arise.
5. After reading a message or affirmation: close the eyes, have a full breath, and repeat the statement silently within.
6. After reading a message or affirmation: visualize and feel a specific situation, or life in general being better.

Each message matches the following affirmation.
Each page can also be reflected upon independently.

Graceful Reflection

There is only one Reflection seen through many mirrors.

Reflection through Self

Reflection through Self

For reasons beyond
my perception,
I am here.

I AM ETERNAL.

A moment of surrender;
I cannot control thoughts.

I AM CALM.

Reflection through Self

I only *see* what I *feel*.
Perception is created
through
the lenses of emotion.

I AM CO-CREATING.

Human beings are the cells of the Planet.
I am glad to be Healthy.

I AM CONTRIBUTING.

Reflection through Self

To some, I'm going to be the Hero.
To some, I'm going to be the Villain.
I embrace every Role.

I AM AN ILLUSION.

Reflection through Self

I think I am helping everyone,
but everyone is helping me.

Graceful Reflection

I AM ABLE.

Reflection through Self

I am to be the change I want to see in life.
If I want life to relax, then I must relax.
If I want life to shift, then I must shift.

I AM POSSIBILITY.

Reflection through Self

It takes Great Courage
to implement
Self Love.

Graceful Reflection

I AM CARING.

Things are doable
from the
Right Perspective.

I AM PROGRESSING.

To be in the world,
but not of the world;
I am open to discover my Truth.

I AM LIBERATION.

Reflection through Self

Duality,
accepting both sides
of
my Self.

I AM FORGIVENESS.

Reflection through Self

I have a lot of Abundance.

Graceful Reflection

I AM ABUNDANCE.

Reflection through Self

Wealth continues to flow
whether
I acknowledge it or not.

I AM PROSPEROUS.

Reflection through Self

Anything
I love
or hate,
I see within
my Self.

I AM COMPASSION.

Reflection through Self

I am a Superb Receiver,
so that I am a Superb Giver.

I AM RECIPROCAL.

Reflection through Self

I
"Yes"
every
day.

I AM INSPIRATION.

It is a gift to cry.

I AM HEALING.

Reflection through Self

It is a gift to cry.

I AM JOYFUL.

I love
the Sound of Thought.

Graceful Reflection

I AM EASE.

Reflection through Love

Reflection through Love

I love me, so yes, I love you.

I AM REFLECTIVE.

Reflection through Love

As a partner, my heart has equal value.
(note to self.)

I AM VALUABLE.

Reflection through Love

I do hate you.
So, yes, I hate that part of myself.

Graceful Reflection

I AM ACCOUNTABLE.

...both my Masculinity and Femininity needed some Healing.

I AM DUALITY.

Reflection through Love

I can't force someone to love me
by the things I do or have done.
I have to allow space for love
to naturally flow and be.

I can't force Self Love onto myself
by the things I do or have done.
I have to allow space for love
to naturally flow and be.

I AM ALLOWING.

Reflection through Love

Everything presents an opportunity
to reflect Beauty.
Even Separation, can show
the Strength of Connection.

I AM GROWING.

Reflection through Love

Hearing is one thing,
Listening is another.

I AM PRESENCE.

She/he is not the Right Partner,
but
she/he is the Right Teacher.

I AM BENEFITING.

Our purpose is greater than
I can conceive.

I AM HUMILITY.

Reflection through Love

I am finally Conscious
of the Unconscious Role
I played.

I AM EVOLVING.

Reflection through Love

No words can accurately describe a feeling.

I AM RADIANT.

Reflection through Love

I was trying to prove or earn love,
rather than Being Loving itself.

Graceful Reflection

I AM WISE.

Reflection through Love

I do Love, and now I Trust.

I AM SHIFTING.

Reflection through Love

We balance each other.

I AM FULFILLING.

Reflection through Love

We are a Vibrational Match.

I AM A FREQUENCY.

Instead of being Born into Sin,
what if I was Born into a Blessing?

I AM SAFE.

Reflection through God

The Universal Spirit
is
Listening.

I AM A PRAYER.

When bliss knocks,
the door is open.

I AM AFFIRMING.

Reflection through God

Shifting from "beware" to Be Aware.

I AM COURAGE.

Everything is a Path.

I AM SACRED.

Reflection through God

Accepting a Loss oddly feels like a Gain.

I AM RECEIVING.

Trust the Future.
Trust the Now.

I AM FAITH.

Money is Spiritual.

Graceful Reflection

I AM RICH.

Reflection through God

The world is full of Mirrors.

I AM OMNIPOTENT.

Reflection through God

Miracles happen
in everyday Life.

I AM MIRACULOUS.

Reflection through God

The love I have for myself
gets reflected through different people.

I AM OBSERVING.

The concept
that Light = Good
and Dark = Evil
is Fictitious.

I AM BALANCE.

Reflection through God

Through my parents, I see the world.

I AM LEGACY.

My Plan A was to win the lottery.
Now it is time for the Universe's Plan A.

I AM A DIVINE PLAN.

Reflection through God

I have things to complain about,
and
I have things to express gratitude for.

I AM NEUTRAL.

Spirit is similar to the wind;
I feel it,
see things move,
and am certain It is there.

I AM CONSCIOUS.

Reflection through God

Thank you for appearing,
and being present.

I AM GRATITUDE.

...THIS is Spiritual for me.

I AM ENERGY.

Seek you, the Kingdom of God, first.

I AM GOD'S IMAGE.

Reflection through God

Once I can accept that I am God,
I can also accept that I am in Heaven.

I AM THAT I AM.

Reflection through God

What is a church without people?
What is a person without a message?
The body is a temple.

I AM
THE LIVING WORD.

Much Grace, Gratitude, and Appreciation

Visit

www.jameseditor.com

or

James Editor

on

Facebook

YouTube

Twitter

Soundcloud

www.ingramcontent.com/pod-product-compliance
Lightning Source LLC
Chambersburg PA
CBHW042127100526
44587CB00026B/4207